Empty Your Cup

EMPTY YOUR CUP

c. martins

Table of Contents

Chosen disposition

Happiness
can it be sought
can it be bought

Can it persist
can it only exist
in hindsight
while searching with a flashlight
will it slip through your fingers
if you hold on too tight

Why does it always appear
like a distant destination
rather than residing
in your habitual location

Why does it seem
like a goal out of reach
why isn't it something
that a professor can teach

Maybe it doesn't happen by chance
maybe it's independent of circumstance

Instead maybe it's your choice
to make it your constant disposition
finding reason to rejoice
regardless of outer conditions

Outburst

Anger is loud
anger is a shout
anger is someone saying cut that out

Anger is unpredictable
patience on a thread
we know someone is angry
when they lose their head

Anger takes aim
an arrow of fire
don't fan the flame
don't get caught in the crossfire

There can be feelings
of loss of control
like a train running off course
a powerful force

Maybe the antidote
is to watch
the spectacle of our angry outburst
as spectators
watch as the toxic fumes
affect everyone in the room

We can refuse to engage in warfare
disarming anger by becoming more aware
after all, if you look in anger's eyes
you'll see sadness in disguise

New moon

Feeling low
so-called dark nights of the soul

You question your life
and seek a direction
and ponder the possibility
you're obsessed with perfection

This is the time
you get down on your knees
and pray to a deity
or another granter of peace

It's likely
the answers you seek are within
and no decision
should be made in the interim

It's not the time
to make promises to keep
you'll need a period
of rest and sleep

Sleep for the body
rest for the soul
space for a mind
that feels out of control

Next best step
feel this phase through
feel to break through
allowing what you seek to find you

Fight or flight

Fear is a yellow fellow
his urge is to run
from every new thing under the sun
he abhors novelty
his level of scrutiny
provides a false sense of security

Panic
feels like you're under attack
the mind is sequestered
there's loss of common sense
and heightened bodily sense

Body overtaken by fear
knees buckle
heart starts to race
drenched in cold sweat
at the thought of disgrace

Fear begets fear
paralysis through analysis
feeling loss of control
whenever fear take hold

Fear tests your commitment to your desire
courage is what's required
as love and fear cannot coexist
fear is love's antagonist

Human kind

Compassion is an outstretched hand
in troubled times
an ear to lend

It's a glimmer of hope in the dark
it's the kind word we're willing to impart

It's empathy in action
a heartfelt reaction
to the plight of another
a sister, a brother

It serves as consolation
in desperate situations

When you're in a dire circumstance
you may isolate yourself
and feel alone in a pack
the weight of the world on your back

We all share feeling isolated
in difficult situations
may we share more feelings
in our communications

Maybe time alone mends wounds
with healing more likely later than soon

Since we don't wear our thoughts on our sleeve
we may be unaware when another feels grief

Because we're blind
let us be as we're designed
human kind

Walk in my shoes

Sometimes I walk in other people's shoes
any type of shoe
I wear different shoes for different views

In high heels
I walk tall
but my feet feel so small
I can hardly walk at all

Old sneakers are comfy
but they're in bad shape
undervalued and overused
holes covered with tape

Some shoes can only be used
at a specific time
like the trusty rainboot
forgotten in sunshine

Some shoes are too big
to walk in the street
I must walk carefully
to not step on other feet

Sometimes I put on the glasses of others
some come in different colors
some allow more light to shine through
some give a worldview in a new hue

We wear shoes for protection
to shield our feet when we run
we wear glasses for protection
to shield our eyes from the sun

These extra layers we wear
underneath we are bare
may we be fearless there
and remember
we choose what we wear

Let it be

People disappoint us
a fact we must learn to accept
we may be triggered
because it's hard to forget

If time is an illusion
then the past is present
and when we react
the past is present

We can't erase what we think we know
about familiar people, places, and things
feelings remain with us
attached by invisible strings

But must we repeat the past ad eternum?
only if we choose to remain numb

Maybe the lesson is
to accept each person and thing
let it be is the verse we should sing

Although it seems strange
it's the only way things change
we set the stage when we disengage

By accepting that everyone is free
by a willingness to agree to disagree

We grow up with the story of the hero
we hope to be saved in the end
but we're here to save ourselves
to evolve, transcend, and amend

Mirror

Every time you speak to someone you know
especially those you've known a long time
there's a preconceived idea of who they are in your mind
try speaking to them as if for the first time

People are as wonderful or hateful
as the part we create for them to play

What's your preconceived notion of me?
one thing you can be certain of
I am always and only that which you think I am

The me that you imagine me to be
only exists in relation to you
or maybe we are one and the same
I'm a mirror held up for you

Thoughts like stories

Was your mind with you all day today
did you notice some thoughts were replayed
thoughts like stories
stories like

There isn't enough time
for all I need to claim
there's so much crime
and it's such a shame

That things aren't different
they shouldn't be this way
I need more
but I must save for a rainy day

There's no point in trying
it's all been done before
no one does what they want
that's what work's for

Joy and happiness are temporary
and things aren't like they used to be
back then it was better
deterioration is the tendency

Thoughts are stories
that we create from what we see
or might it be
that our world mirrors our beliefs

Mental maze

Lost in thought
lost in abstraction
feeling distraught
unnecessary distraction

Fortress of thoughts
that leads to obsession
like a fever you caught
thoughts in rapid succession

You lose sight of the day
you lose sight of the night
looking for reason
with reason nowhere in sight

Like when you can't see
the forest for the trees
tree for the leaves
heart for the chest
girl for the dress
words for the page
wisdom for the age
mind for the brain
love for the pain

A.I.

The mind is a machine
primed to organize our routine
taking myriad data of our lives
and fitting it into a single serving size

Memories are files
saved in orderly piles
compact version of all data compiled

We are our memories
a repertory of sensory reveries
a mental summary of our legacies
who would you be without your memory

Artificial intelligence is the tip of the glacier
while enigmatic emotions reveal our true nature
like a bland dish, it's the spice that adds flavor

Automated mind machine
same thoughts playing on our mental screen

Some thoughts on the conveyor belt
in our mental factory
must be recalled
or risk being refractory

Forgotten

Memory is a paradox
you only know you forget
when you remember you forgot

If it's on the tip of your tongue
and can't be released
maybe it wasn't a relevant piece

Memory is a slippery slope
something slips your mind
forgotten because it's remote

We think the world sees and remembers our blunders
but it's forgotten by the world the moment after
every mistake, every fall
may we be like the world that forgets mistakes, one and all

What a joy to forget all blunders that have no part to play
may you always remember that the world forgets everyday
may you forget in this way as the world forgets everyday
may you forget the world in the best way everyday

Scars

Do we need to remember
or do we need to forget
every instance of time
that we deeply regret

We remember our past
all the moments we feel
we get hurt and get scars
scars that must heal

Inscribed on the body
inscribed on the heart
if it had an impact
it left an indelible mark

Rainy days to value
the return of the sun
then spend our time
pretending they're done

Resilience or trauma
it's a fine line
but you're master of your fate
captain of your storyline

Storm

Why run from the rain
rain is indispensable
and getting wet is inevitable

Maybe rain
helps us appreciate the sun
but when you're in a storm
you can't wait 'til it's done

Rather than regret getting wet
maybe you'll see the good in it yet
maybe to feel more sun when it's done

Let go of what you know

We all have memories
some good
some regrettable
but regret is pointless
it proves they remain unforgettable

If we're products of our past
and all we have is the present
by remaining intentionally present
may we, in essence, be changing the past?

Memories are our interpretation
of what happened long ago
we can choose what we remember
and we can choose what we let go

You need not forget all you know
you need only create some distance
so that what you think you know
can become what you choose to forgo

Stereotype

I had a dream
of the most beautiful bird
like the bird I heard
singing his song
on one of the best days
heralding a new beginning
since then, all birds are beautiful

You had a dream
of a mischievous bird
like the bird that swooped in for a bite of your meal
that he thought he could steal
since then, all birds must be kept under watchful eye

Our experiences help shape our views
memories are revisited and recycled
or maybe we choose to see anew

Cloud 9

Returning to a favorite place
like a favorite scent you can trace
you remember every feeling, every face

You fall in love with a place
like falling in love with a person
slowly at first
and then all of a sudden

You're both spectator
and playing the leading part
like live props that engage
the moment you step on the stage

Unknown parts of you awaken
becoming more alive in action
like noticing your feet when you move them
a welcome escape from abstraction

Empty your cup

Open mind means accepting
you get what you see
while seeing beyond faces
especially in new places

Open mind is flexible
releasing all you expect
open mind attempts
to keep feelings in check

Open mind means
there's room for surprises
it requires acceptance
of all that arises

Open mind
empty cup
necessary condition
to be filled up

So empty your cup
before you go
ergo it won't overflow

Nine lives

Curiosity is not to blame for the cat's demise
rather it's the reason the cat has nine lives

Curiosity is the beginning
of everything worthwhile
if you're curious
then you're likely versatile

It's a sign of attention
it's a sign of affection

If it piques your curiosity
it may be wise to invest
as it may pay dividends
you may even gain interest

Follow your curiosity
it won't lead you astray
it's always a gift
connecting tomorrow to today

Prolific

Inspiration
lady of creative liberty
lucky he who can be
in the same vicinity as she

She's prolific
long tresses for a mane
that act to transmit
ideas to other brains

She takes bits and pieces
we pick up along the way
helping to smooth out the creases
creating art to portray

She arrives unannounced
so leave the door wide open
to not risk a missed visit
her value unspoken

She's open-minded
ready try something new
whispering thoughts to others
conveying new views to a select few

She's most humble
never asking for recognition
for the role that she plays
disinhibition of intuition

Some writers fear the moment
she'll disappear from their lives
but in fact you need only
summon for her to arrive

Bubble

Life in a bubble
what a good place to be
or so it may seem
a life with more tranquility

Protected but distanced
you don't feel extremes
but it makes you miss out
on the sweet in between

All experiences neutral
living life on the surface
having less options
but nothing can hurt us

Bubbles seem better
but bubbles can pop
what's real makes you feel
what's real can't be topped

Hush

Silence
a precious commodity
needed for concentration and rest
allowing novel ideas to be expressed

Its presence or absence can indicate plenty
it's silent discomfort if you're with someone new
or with someone you know
it's an enjoyable interlude

It can feel like a warm embrace
or it can feel limiting
like lack of space

It can feel eerie
like silence before a storm
or it can make you feel reassured
like a friend who doesn't conform

At night it can be deafening
and appear rather threatening
in the day it can be a relief
when intervals of silence are brief

Silence holds
thoughts and feelings
silence can be filled
with music, laughter, tears, and meaning

Silence is space
to think, feel, and be
silence is invaluable
a forerunner of serenity

Nightly interlude

What is it about the night
that makes us pensive
that makes worries bubble to the surface
making us feel apprehensive

Lost memories may return
unannounced and uninvited
unrest that we must unlearn

The moon
like the silence and the night
bears witness to all
we keep hidden from the light

Silence is the beginning and the end
it can lead to unease
but it can also be a friend
as a silent mind provides protection
from unnecessary introspection

The moon reminds us
to stay hopeful
no matter how long-lasting the night appears
as each visit by the moon
is a sign that dawn is near

Impermanence

Everything is temporary
some things persist longer than others
we're aware of our mortality
it's a game of numbers

We want to be unaware
of this truth so difficult to bear
that impermanence is a fate we all share

Despite our temporary condition
we seek to connect
creating bonds that bind us
pretending to forget
that the day to say goodbye will find us
may we have no regrets

We're merely mortal
our lives a short interval
we choose daily distractions
a means of abstraction

If only we could live from the end
decisions contingent
on the provisional state of affairs
maybe we'd take more risks
and be more aware

Remembering that everything is at stake
we might be willing to make more mistakes

Everything imbued with meaning
and everyone imbued with feelings
maybe that's what it means to be human 'beings'

Refuge

Feeling of belonging
like the feeling of returning home
your feet instinctively know where to go
every detail permanently engraved in your memory

There's no feeling
quite like the feeling
of returning home
especially when home is your world
especially when your world moves
to a distant point
at a critical point
when you were shaping your worldview

Maybe difficult times provide depth
depth of being
depth of feeling
you appreciate everything
and take nothing for granted

Becoming aware of the limits of time
each moment is the first and last time
because you're more present when it's the first time
because you're more present when you know it's the last time

Diamond

In an awakened dream
it became clear

All the things we struggle with
our sensitivities
all add to our gift

Like a diamond formed under pressure
all struggles act like a chisel
revealing our purpose

Peer pressure

As you progress up the ladder of success
a never-ending staircase of steps
ambition can lead to praises and gains
to justify your labor pains

Adding fuel to the fire of ambition
but making you question your volition

If we measure our success
based on social status and position
we'll forever be in competition
feeling inadequate despite outward recognition

Constant striving puts us at risk
of losing our self-identity
becoming a puppet
a nonentity

Each person is singular
unique in mind and tastes
born into a family, creed, and race
each will have different dreams to chase

May you redefine real success
as personal satisfaction in the dreams you possess
your dreams are not mere coincidence

Balloon

Aim high
dreams like pie in the sky

A dream is a balloon
that well-meaning words can perforate
causing it to deflate
along with your mood

Like a balloon that floats
when you let go of the strand
do the same with your dream
and open your hand

It's in letting go
that the dream can take flight
though it seems out of reach
your dream is your birthright

On the way

On the way
to where I'm going
I'll take the time
to smell the flowers
since these are the only flowers I can smell
in this place
and at this time
and they've never smelled so sweet
as they do here
in this place
and at this time

Ferris wheel

Life is a ferris wheel
the biggest ride at the fair
towering over the others
not all regard it as fair

Life is a ferris wheel
a ride you must take
a feeling of trepidation
as you await your meeting with fate

You begin at the bottom
you learn as you go
the wheel spins and you climb
front-row seats to the show

The view at the top is breathtaking
a feeling of awe
followed quickly by the thought
what if I fall

The wheel keeps spinning
first you're down then you're up
wondering the whole time
when will my time be up

Life is a wheel of fortune
you take a roll of the dice
always spinning, always changing
no time to think twice

The wheel of life waits for no one
you blink and it passed
so don't spin on a whim
enjoy the ride while it lasts

Note from the author

Thanks for reading.

If you enjoyed this book,
please consider leaving a review on Amazon:
https://a.co/d/gBPAHDv

For more poetry and news on upcoming books,
visit www.cmartinspoetry.com.

www.ingramcontent.com/pod-product-compliance
Lightning Source LLC
Chambersburg PA
CBHW070556160726
48003CB00005B/2072